ON

ARTIFICIAL LIMBS

THEIR

CONSTRUCTION AND APPLICATION.

BY

HENRY HEATHER BIGG,

ANATOMICAL, SURGICAL, AND ORTHOPŒDIC

MECHANICIAN

TO THE

GOVERNMENT HOSPITALS OF CHELSEA AND GREENWICH;
THE ADMIRALTY, EAST INDIA COMPANY,
BOARD OF ORDNANCE, ST. GEORGE'S, MIDDLESEX, GUYS, ST. THOMAS'S
UNIVERSITY, KING'S COLLEGE, ROYAL FREE HOSPITALS, ETC.

LONDON:
JOHN CHURCHILL, NEW BURLINGTON STREET.
MDCCCLV.

This scarce antiquarian book is included in our special *Legacy Reprint Series*. In the interest of creating a more extensive selection of rare historical book reprints, we have chosen to reproduce this title even though it may possibly have occasional imperfections such as missing and blurred pages, missing text, poor pictures, markings, dark backgrounds and other reproduction issues beyond our control. Because this work is culturally important, we have made it available as a part of our commitment to protecting, preserving and promoting the world's literature. Thank you for your understanding.

TO THE

Members of the Medical Profession

The following pages are respectfully dedicated by one who, attributing entirely to their recommendation and kind instruction, the experience necessary for the successful pursuit of his particular calling, takes this opportunity of recording his grateful thanks for past favors, and sanguine expectations of their future continuance.

PREFACE.

At a time, like the present, when the vicissitudes inseparable from War are largely adding to the number of that class of the community who, even in order to fulfil the simple requirements of daily life, are compelled to have recourse to artificial aid, a few remarks explanatory of the nature and form of various mechanical substitutes for natural limbs, accompanied by a description of the scientific principles involved in their construction, the method of their application, and advantage possessed by one particular kind over another for special purpose, may not be altogether undeserving of notice. Few persons, unless made acquainted by practical experience with the difficulty of successfully imitating the mechanical action of a leg or an arm, can be at all aware of the extreme pains-taking and care with which every movement simulated must be studied. In ordinary contrivance it is simply requisite to consider the end to be attained, and then render the means subservient, but where the needed apparatus is of an anatomical character, and must strictly be conformed to certain symmetric proportion, sometimes at apparent mechanical variance with the point to be accomplished, the difficulty of construction is considerably increased. To prove this it is only necessary to examine a natural leg, and suppose its shape superficially followed in the formation of a mechanical substitute, the result of which would be that when needed for use, instead of offering support capable of sustaining the *weight* of the human body, it would yield in its joints the moment such weight was applied, the reason being that the *actual* centres of motion differ from their *apparent* external position.

In the form of the knee joint, for instance, the motion is not, as would at first be imagined, derivable from a point in the middle of the knee, but has its existence at least half an inch behind such supposed centre, the action resembling a hinge, with the patella, or knee cap, covering the open or basal extremity. Thus, anatomically and osteologically, the centre is not in the place it would appear to be, when the leg is only superficially observed or considered in an artistic light.

Although less in amount, difficulties likewise attend the construction of artificial substitutes for the upper extremity, or arms ; but in the following pages every obstacle opposed to the exercise of mechanical ingenuity will be found not only fully described, but scientifically explained and overcome.

29, *Leicester Square, London.*

CONTENTS.

PART I.

Preface v

CHAPTER I.

Mechanism applied as a substitute for natural limbs—Anatomical form, condition, and required mechanical length of stump—Province of the mechanician, &c.—Artificial leg above knee—New and important principle in the form of bucket or stump-sheath—Bucket, or common wooden leg—Kneeling leg . . 1

CHAPTER II.

Legs above knee—Point where the weight of body should rest—Line of gravity in the stump—Artificial limbs obedient to natural mechanical law—Case in illustration of contracted stump—Successful application of artificial leg, and letter from the patient 11

CHAPTER III.

On the mechanical position of the articulations or joints—Action of knee-joint—Mechanical power employed—Action of ankle-joint 19

CHAPTER IV.

Leg below knee—Box or common wooden leg—Improved box leg—Socket leg—Artificial or shaped leg—Short stump—Slender stump—Conservative surgery—Chopard's operation—Form of artificial foot—Surface upon which the body should rest—Stump cap for relieving pressure against knee—Mechanical removal of rectangular contraction in stump —Case—Treatment—Mechanism employed—Successful application of two artificial legs 26

PART II.

CHAPTER I.

Introductory remarks—Artificial hands and arms—

CONTENTS. xi

Novel plan for gaining finger motion by a column of mercury—Artificial arms—Form of stump—Conical stump—Stump thickened at its end—Best form of stump for mechanical attachment. . . 43

CHAPTER II.

Various contrivances employed after amputation of stump above elbow—Improved shape of stump sheath—Angular motion at elbow joint—Excision of arm at shoulder joint—Arms below elbow—Form of sheath —Common arm—Short stump and apparatus—Conservative surgery—Preservation of articular surfaces —Amputation of thumb or fingers—apparatus. 51

CHAPTER III.

Artificial fingers and hand—Mechanical motion—Form of hand—softening of surface—Form of joint—Ginglymoid joint described—Position of mechanical axes in fingers and thumb—Form of wrist—Spring in thumb joint. 61

CHAPTER IV.

Instruments for artificial hand—Hook—Driving hook— Holding gun—Lifting weights—Fork for holding

CONTENTS.

food—Pen-holder—Nail brush—Penknife—Ring for spade or agricultural implements—Dagger or weapon for defence—Instructions for taking measure of leg or arm—Conclusion. 68

ON
ARTIFICIAL LIMBS,
&c.

PART I.

CHAPTER I.

Mechanism applied as a substitute for natural limbs—Anatomical form, condition, and required mechanical length of stump—Province of the mechanician, &c.—Artificial leg above knee—New and important principle in the form of bucket or stump-sheath—bucket, or common wooden leg—Kneeling leg.

WHEN from accident or disease it has become advisable to have the whole or a part of the natural leg removed by the knife of the surgeon, the first thought invariably arising in a patient's mind is how he can possibly walk and pursue his usual avocation when minus a limb.

Difficult as the matter appears, it is by no means too much so for human ingenuity to accomplish, and various mechanical substitutes have from the earliest times been devised for the purpose of supplying the place of the excised member. Whatever their constructive form, the end and aim in all such pieces of mechanism is to find a substitute for the handywork of nature; but as it requires the exercise of great skill and much ingenuity to approach within the widest limit of anything so exquisitely contrived as the human frame, the clumsiest imaginable apparati are occasionally resorted to : such, for instance, as a mere rest for the stump and a pin or stick to make up its distance from the ground. The perfection of mechanical ingenuity applied to such a purpose is when the substitute constructed to represent a natural limb has its form and action in strict accordance with the anatomical condition of the remaining leg. It is, therefore, clearly the part of the "mechanician" to render himself acquainted with the anatomical details of the limb he has to imitate, and also ascertain any peculiar action by which the various joints are brought into motion or sustained at rest. It is likewise his province to take into consideration the different lengths of stump and consequent modification required in the adaptation of his scientific contrivances. Without a correct understanding of this latter important point all mere imitative effort is certain to prove unavailing and entail discredit.

It must not, however, be supposed that the length of the remaining portion of leg, or stump, is always a matter of choice, even to the surgeon, as the existence of an extensively diseased surface frequently renders an operation necessary that involves a loss of nearly the entire limb. In adjusting an artificial leg, speed in acquiring its use greatly depends upon the amount of stump remaining ; though, if the distance from its upper part to its end be but a few inches, mechanical means are fortunately available by which a leg can be attached. It is needless, however, to remark that the difficulty of obtaining a fixed point is greatly increased by want of a good and lengthy surface. In amputation above knee, the best length the stump can possess (for the mechanician) is when two-thirds of the thigh remain, more than this only involving a possibility of the anterior end being pressed against the front of the bucket or thigh-sheath when the patient commences walking, which, besides creating a feeling of pain, tends to *unfix* the perpendicular line assumed by the leg when the limb is thrown forward, as acting below the middle of the bucket, it enters into the leverage belonging to the knee-joint, and brings it unduly into action. For a leg below knee the length of stump is *not* a matter of such extreme importance, although if it be shorter than one-third, mechanical attachment of the leg to the thigh, by means of lateral metal stems jointed at the knee, becomes necessary to impart the required leverage, and prevent the weight of the leg from loosening its hold upon the stump. In the following pages a description will be given of what is required not only to ensure accuracy of fit, but perfection of anatomical detail. To prevent any miscomprehension of terms, it is well to remember the two principal forms of artificial leg, viz., where the amputation has taken place in any part of the thigh, the leg is called "artificial leg above knee," and after amputation of any part of the leg or foot "artificial leg below knee," the modification of these two kinds of legs have different names, which will be found under their respective headings.

ARTIFICIAL LEG ABOVE KNEE.

An artificial leg above knee, when properly constructed, represents in external form the shape of the remaining limb, and equally corresponds in articular action. Its mode of attachment to the stump is by means of a hollowing of its thigh or bucket, and its joints are brought into motion either by the action of the stump—as at the knee—or by metallic and other springs as at the ankle and toe joints.

Upon the fit of the bucket and the anatomical accuracy of the joints depends the fulfilment of its intended purpose. If the conditions required for its perfect construction are fully complied with, the form and action of the leg will be found almost as natural as the opposite limb; and cases have frequently occurred within the experience of the writer where detection of the false leg from the real by a visual observer has been a matter of considerable difficulty.

For the purpose of assisting the reader to understand the different parts of an artificial leg referred to in the following pages, a drawing of one above knee is appended, with a description of its technicalities.

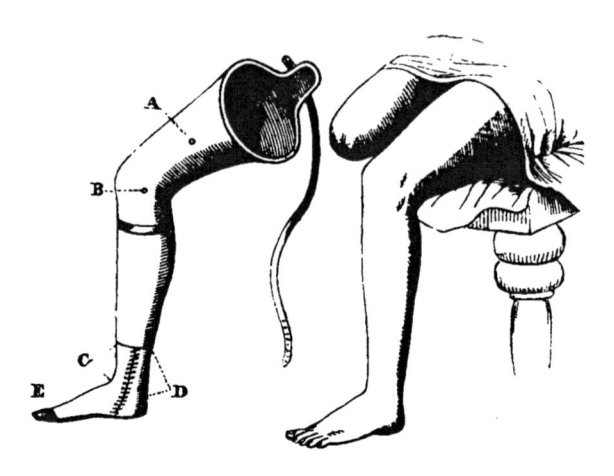

A, bucket; B, knee-bolt; C, instep spring; D, back spring; E, toe-joint.

The bucket is that portion of the artificial leg which receives the stump. Upon its perfect construction entirely depends the action and stability of the remaining parts. The writer has recently discovered and applied a new principle to the formation of this important surface; the value of which it is impossible to over-estimate, as whilst it enables the most perfect apposition to be maintained between the stump and its artificial receptacle, only *one* actual point of bearing is employed—in exact conformity with the internal anatomy of the limb. The bolts are the various articular centres required to fix the different parts of the artificial leg together and produce axial motion. The springs are the mock muscles, or motors governing the action of the ankle and toe-joints. The stump is the remaining portion of the natural leg.

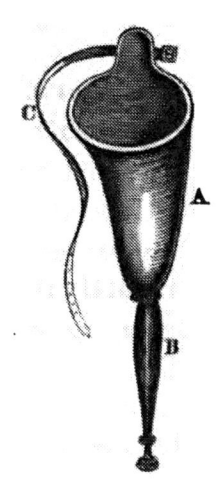

It may be as well likewise to describe the shape and form of an ordinary bucket leg, such, in fact, as is usually made use of by the poorest people. It consists, like its more valuable representative, of a hollow sheath or bucket accurately conformed to the shape of the stump, and having—in lieu of the more symmetric proportions of the artificial leg—a pin placed at its lower end to ensure connection between it and the ground.

This form of leg is strongly to be recommended where expense is any object, as it really fulfils all the conditions (excepting external similitude) embraced by a better piece of mechanism. It is likewise occasionally employed with benefit by those patients who from lack of confidence or presence of nervousness prefer learning to use a leg by first practising with the commonest substitute.

There are fewer varieties in legs above knee than below, from the point of amputation rarely differing in the former, but admitting of much deviation in the latter; thus, when a limb is lost above knee, the usual point for surgical removal is about the middle third of the thigh, the stump resulting having an almost universal form and length, but when the limb is amputated below knee, it depends greatly upon the opinion held by the surgeon (as to the most advantageous stump) whether the remaining portion embraces nearly the whole of the tibia or terminates a little below the knee. Two kinds of leg above knee have already had description; there is yet a third which possesses a certain amount of merit, from being less expensive than a complete form of artificial limb, and more useful than the common bucket leg. It consists of a wooden stump sheath furnished with a knee joint, the action of which is entirely under the control of the patient, who can at will produce genuflection or maintain perfect rigidity in the

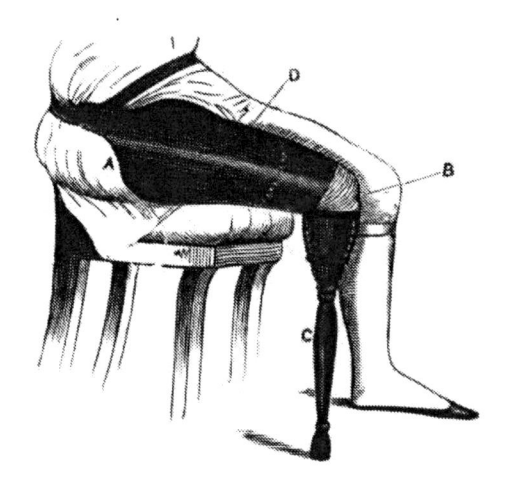

A, Bucket; B, knee-joint; C, pin; D, lever uplifting ratchet-catch at knee.

perpendicular line of the leg. The mechanism employed is a vertical spring bolt and ratchet, which by reference to the preceding diagram may be better understood than if attempted to be described by a lengthy statement of its construction.

CHAPTER II.

Legs above knee—Point where the weight of the body should rest—Line of gravity in the stump—Artificial limbs obedient to natural mechanical law—Case in illustration of contracted stump—Successful application of artificial leg, and letter from the patient.

THE primary object entertained in the construction of a substitute for the natural limb is to place the weight of the trunk on such portions of the artificial surface as are most mechanically enabled to assist locomotion without imparting any painful pressure to that part of the body to which it is attached, viz., the stump. This point, until recently made the subject of close investigation, had scarcely ever been viewed other than as capable of accomplishment by the mere handy work of the artisan, regardless altogether of osteologic configuration.

No error could, however, have been fraught with worse results, as may be learnt from the numerous failures attending the use of unscientific contrivances.

In order to explain more fully the advantages accruing from carefully selecting particular points of bearing, it may suffice to state that if after amputation above knee a stump thinly covered by integument remaining, a mere bucket or hollow wooden sheath were adjusted, regardless of anything but conformity to external shape, the effect would be to draw the flesh upwards and produce, not only painful, but injurious pressure at the end of stump. Whereas, were that portion of the stump called the tuberosity of the ischium,* selected for the principal point of resistance, and the remaining part of the bucket left free, the patient would with ease rest the whole weight of his body upon the false leg without in the slightest degree uplifting the fleshy part of the stump. In constructing an artificial leg above the knee, therefore, the following scientific principles

---

* The tuberosity of the ischium is a bony prominence easily felt at the back part of the thigh, and upon which the body rests whilst sitting down.

(which admit of easy elucidation) have to be considered:—first, that the centre of gravity, or that perpendicular line by which the weight of the patient's body must be evenly borne, is in the same position as where nature places it in the original limb; and secondly, that the articulations or joints are so formed as not only to yield to the leverage exercised by the stump for the purpose of walking, but maintain the leg in a perpendicular position when the gravity or weight of the artificial limb alone brings them into action.

To discover the precise spot where the centre

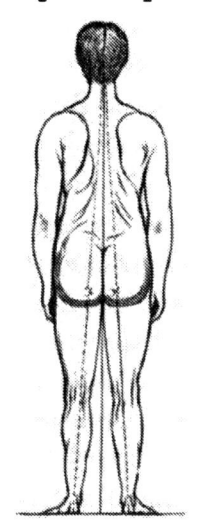

of gravity exists, reference must be made to the foregoing diagram, which represents in rough outline the pelvis and shape of the natural limb.

A dotted line passes down the centre of each leg and terminates in the head,—this illustrates the centre of gravity in each limb when the weight of the body is placed upon either, as in the act of walking. It will be perceived that, from the breadth of the pelvis, these lines merely approximate slightly,—their point for commingling being in the head,—which thus forms the apex of a triangle. Now if any one will carefully examine a skeleton, and contrast it with a living person, they will find that in the pelvis, where the lines in the drawing approach nearer than at their base, and at the back of the thigh, a hard bony prominence may be felt which is called the tuberosity of the ischium, and it is through this point that the mechanical line enabling the figure to be held upright when borne upon one leg passes. It must be understood that the dotted lines simply describe the centre of gravity pertaining to *each* limb,—that which corresponds to the whole body is the dark vertical line drawn from the head to the middle of a base formed by both legs. During the act of walking, the point created by the perpendicular position of the body deviates from the middle of the base just mentioned, and alternately falls within the sole of each foot, forming part of the line marked by dots in the diagram.

From this it will be at once seen that in the construction of the bucket of an artificial leg only one spot exists where the bearing of the body can be correctly placed, which, if clearly understood by the "mechanician," enables him to render the construction of the remaining portion a matter of comparative simplicity.

The right comprehension of this point of bearing against the ischium occasionally becomes a matter of the highest importance, not only in preventing the patient from experiencing the inconvenience of a strained stump, but permitting him to walk at all. To prove which the following case may be adduced.

Mr. W * * *, aged 18, had suffered amputation of his right leg, five inches below the fork or perinæum. Owing to its being improperly supported whilst healing, aided by the prior existence of lumbar curvature of the vertebræ, the stump became contracted laterally and anteriorly, that is, he was unable to bring the thigh in a straight line with the body, or make it touch with its end the opposite leg. It is evident that if an artificial leg were merely attached, on *ordinary* principles, to a stump of this kind, its lower extremity or foot would be several inches in advance of the other, and what is of still greater importance, several inches distant laterally from the opposite foot.

To obviate and overcome difficulties so striking, the limb was merely regarded by the writer as having one point of bearing, around which the stump in contraction had formed a kind of axis. A bucket or wooden sheath was consequently so made as to have its sole point of bearing against the ischium, and a perpendicular line taken from thence to the ground, regardless altogether of the shape and direction of the stump, which was with care merely fitted into the bucket in its contracted position.

Upon the artificial leg being applied, Mr. W * * * stood and walked as perfectly as he would have done had the stump been in a normal condition ; and three weeks afterwards the following letter was received from him :—

"*To Messrs. Bigg, & Co.*

"*April* 21, 1855.

"Gentlemen,

"I BEG to say, that it is with feelings of the greatest satisfaction mingled with pleasure, that I forward (herewith) the balance due to you for the leg which has been so skilfully executed under your practical superintendence.

"Trusting you will receive my sincere thanks for your unremitting attention in removing all obstacles that might obstruct or mar my walking, and hoping YOUR NAME will receive such publicity as it richly deserves.

"I remain, &c.,
"W. W * * *."

Now without a correct knowledge of the only mechanical point of resistance, this leg would have failed as all others he had previously tried to get made had done; in fact, so deeply impressed was the patient with the utter impossibility of making a leg for his particular case, as to propose an arrangement when ordering it, viz., that it should only be paid for on certain conditions, which it is hardly worth while to add were all successfully accomplished.

18 ILLUSTRATION OF CONTRACTED STUMP.

The following diagrams represent the form of the stump, and its position when placed within the artificial leg, the dots showing the line taken from the ischium to the ground.

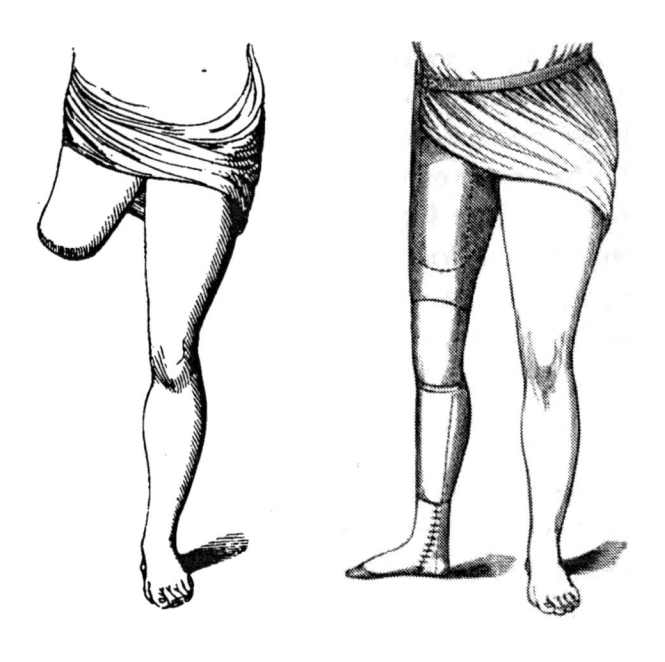

CHAPTER III.

On the mechanical position of the articulations or joints
—Action of knee joint—Mechanical power employed
—Action of ankle joint.

IF the human frame be carefully examined, and reference made to the distribution of such muscular masses as constitute the form and shape of the lower extremities, it will be found that the centre of the knee, the centre of the hip, and the centre of the ankle, are placed rather more towards the *back* part of the limb than the front, by which the joints obtain a hinge-like motion. This will fully account for such powerful muscles as those of the calf and thigh being required to bring into action the joints of the leg. In strict obedience to the example set by nature, the "mechanician" must proceed to construct his artificial articulations, without which, upon the weight of the body being placed upon the leg its centres would yield. If, however, these are scientifically arranged, the weight when added merely serves to increase their stability, as the joints in attempting to bend backwards strengthen themselves, and prevent any anterior yielding. Although nothing in the construction of an artificial leg requires greater care and reflection than the position of the joint centres, it is only during the time the wearer is in a perpendicular posture that they become a matter of high importance: as for the purpose of enabling the patient to progress, the artificial limb must become rigid, which can be alone accomplished by an adherence to the rules just laid down, viz., that the articular centres are so placed as to be behind the line of gravity formed by the weight of the body resting on the artificial surface. To ascertain whether this is rightly carried out or not, it is only necessary to draw a cord from the perinæal edge of the bucket and carry it to the centre of the heel, when the knee-bolt should be three-fourths of an inch, and the ankle-bolt half an inch behind the line so formed.

Having correctly established where the joint centres should be, it becomes requisite to distribute their amount of motion. Various means have been devised for the purpose of governing the knee's action, such as the employment of bands of india-rubber or metallic springs, but either are rendered *unnecessary* if the simple mechanical rule, viz., making the centre a little behind the line of gravity be carefully attended to.

When, however, from shortness of stump or partial paralysis of its muscles, sufficient vigour cannot be imparted to produce anterior action, *then* a special contrivance becomes necessary, and this is best effected in the following manner, a vulcanized india-rubber cord being fixed at one end to the anterior upper edge of the tibial portion of the artificial leg should be reflected over the knee, and passed through a small metal ring like a buckle with its teeth removed, the other end should be carried over the edge of bucket and secured to a shoulder strap : the effect of which is to relieve the stump from the entire backward bearing of the leg when required to be uplifted, and transfer to the shoulder band the power of controlling the action of the leg.

Sometimes, however, it happens, notwithstanding the stump being of proper proportion, that whatever pains the patient takes in learning to gain the natural motion of the knee (whilst walking), his endeavours are in vain, as from a mistaken sense of insecurity the length of swing required to produce a straightening of the knee joint is nervously neglected, and instead of the body depending upon a firm perpendicular prop it has nothing but a yielding support to make use of. When this occurs, and it is impossible to make the patient overcome the badness of his habit, it is requisite to secure the knee by a bolt and thus compel a longer stride on the penalty of tripping at every step.* When the wearer requires to bend the knee for the purpose of sitting down, the bolt is easily withdrawn and the free action of the knee immediately secured.

THE MECHANICAL POWER EMPLOYED TO GIVE MOTION TO THE JOINTS.

NEXT in importance to the position of the

* The stop or bolt consists of a thin strip of steel passing down the side of the leg, and checking the action of the knee joint.

centre of articulations is the mechanical power governing one of their actions, viz. the ankle joints :—and here nature has to be imperfectly followed, as nothing constructed by man has hitherto been found capable of imitating in every respect muscular action. A band of vulcanized india-rubber partially does so, but it is only in one direction, viz., that of its retraction when once extended, but to create an evenness of force by the *suspension* of the withdrawing power of one set of muscles whilst their antagonists are in use, requires nervous vitality and cannot be communicated to inert substances.

To illustrate this it is only necessary to refer to what occurs in bending the arm. During which action the muscles (*biceps flexor cubiti*) placed at the inner and upper surface, and directing the elbow joint, are rendered hard and large, whilst the muscles of the back part of the arm are proportionately relaxed. A great objection to vulcanized bands is that either their elasticity diminishes by frequent use, or they break so frequently as to be a continual plague to the patient, and profit to the leg maker. All this difficulty is obviated by employing a tubular spring, as not only does it exercise retractile

24 ANKLE JOINT AND ITS ACTION.

power when extended, but expansion when compressed, two highly desirable qualities to be combined where equilibrium of centre action has to be maintained.

There cannot be much difficulty in proving that a tubular spring more essentially fulfils the requirements of natural muscular action, than any other plan that can be devised, as it produces contraction and elongation with an evenness of force that nothing else obtains. Besides the vulcanized elastic and tubular spring there is another occasionally employed, which consists

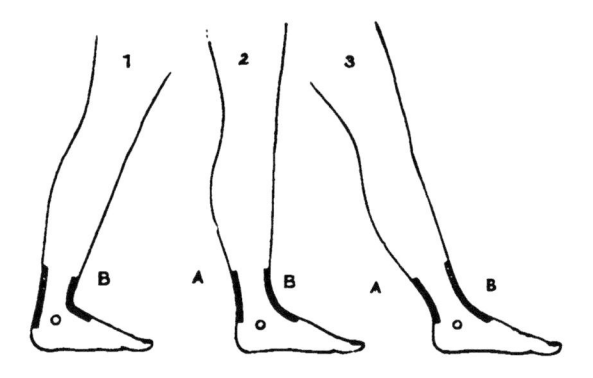

A, represents the back spring, corresponding in form and action to the tendo achillis, or heel tendon; B, the front spring, answering to the peroneii, or those tendons uplifting the front of foot; C. the malleoli, or ankle centre.

of a horizontal slip of metal placed in the sole of the foot, and fastened to the leg part by a catgut band, the elastic reaction of which imparts motion to the ankle joint.

The preceding diagram is framed to show the position in which the tubular springs should be placed, and their relation to the centre of motion.

The object of *every* kind of ankle spring is to elevate the toes : during the time the leg is thrown forward in walking, and allow of their falling when the weight of the body is placed upon the heel, thus securing the appearance of natural action. If this were not carefully attended to, the toes would either strike against every trifling inequality on the surface of the ground, or remain fixed at such an angle, that when the wearer's body became vertical to the leg, they would turn upwards in a grotesque and ridiculous manner.

The third figure in the drawing represents B being elongated, and A, compressed in their helical direction. The former seeks to contract to original dimension, and the latter to expand in similar proportion, thus restoring the foot to its right position.

CHAPTER IV.

Leg below knee—Box or common wooden leg—Improved box leg—Socket leg—Artificial or shaped leg—Short stump—Tender stump—Conservative surgery—Chopard's operation—Form of artificial foot—Surface upon which the body should rest—Stump cap for relieving pressure against knee—Mechanical removal of rectangular contraction in stump—Case—Treatment—Mechanism employed—Successful application of two artificial legs.

HAVING noticed the points requisite to be attended to in the construction of a leg above knee, it follows that some statement should be made of the contrivances which exist for amputation below. Of this kind of artificial leg there are several varieties, the simplest being a common wooden or "box leg," such as may be daily seen in Greenwich Park, on many of the naval pensioners. The form of apparatus merely consists of a hollow trough to receive the knee, a pin to make up its distance from the ground, and a shaft to secure it safely to the wearer's body.

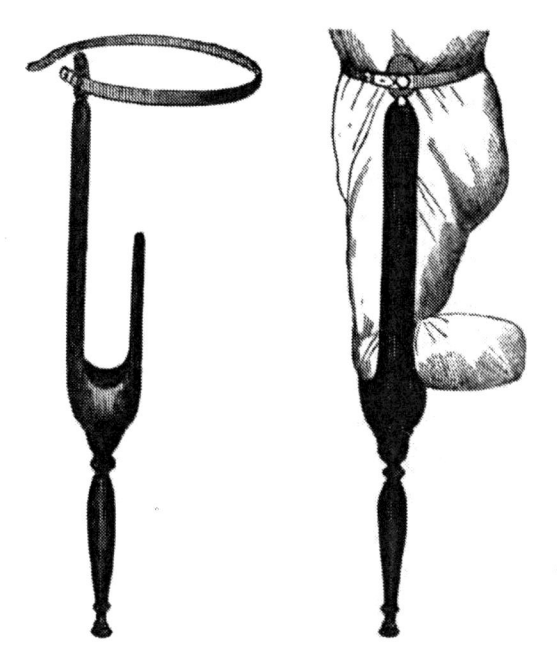

Simple as this kind of mechanical aid undoubtedly is, yet, if properly contrived, there are many conditions in its structure that merit attention. In the first place, the hole into which the pin enters should be bored obliquely, thus widening the base and enabling the patient to stand or walk with greater firmness than if the pin were perpendicular. In addition to this the shaft should be curved a little backwards to conform it with greater perfection to the patient's body. The straps required to fix it should also pass over the woodwork, and *not* through it, by which means closer proximity is secured between the leg and its wearer. An improvement has been introduced by the writer possessing considerable advantage, viz., affixing a perpendicular hinge to the upper end of the leg shaft, which, when the patient sits down, corresponds to the action of the hip joint, and prevents the end of the shaft from thrusting backwards, this hitherto having been the greatest objection attached to the use of a common leg.

Another kind of wooden leg below knee consists of a hollow sheath accurately fitting the stump. This, from the ready suggestion offered by its shape, is called a socket leg, its principal advantage being that it preserves and employs the action of the knee joint, a point too important to be lightly dismissed, as it enables the patient to avoid the awkwardness of upsetting every one, who, not expecting to find a man's leg projecting many inches beyond his chair, accidentally trips against it.

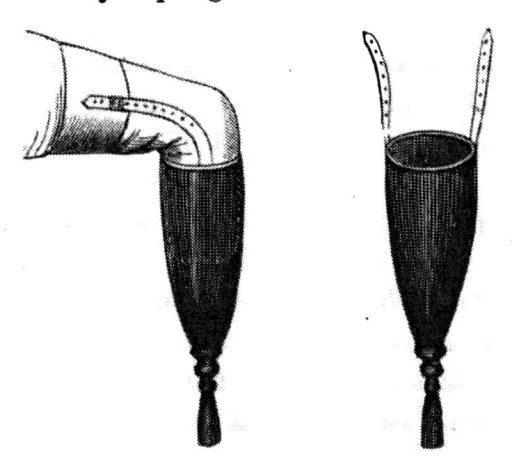

A third kind is the "artificial leg below knee," which has many modifications, all more or less dependent upon the length and condition of the stump, and which requires great care in its skilful construction. If the stump be one third, and its surface strong and healthy, then a sheath terminating at its lower extremity in an ankle and toe joint, and furnished with tubular springs, is the best kind of substitute.

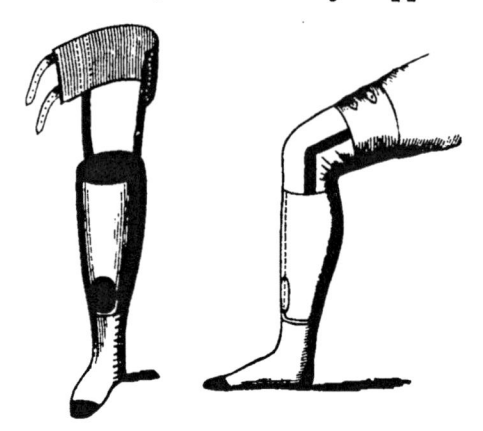

The method by which it is affixed to the leg is by a narrow leathern thigh band and two lateral straps. There cannot be any doubt but what the mechanical point for amputation below knee is a little beneath the junction of the upper and second third of the leg, as it secures at once an useful amount of leverage without creating sufficient length to produce abrasion by rubbing against the inner part of the wooden socket or sheath, as invariably happens if the stump be too long. It has frequently occurred within the writer's experience, that the length of stump has been so great as to necessitate an aperture in the anterior surface of the sheath, as in the foregoing diagram.

Circumstances, however, occasionally arise, requiring the amputation to be above the point heretofore mentioned as the best, leaving often but three inches of stump; when this occurs the same kind of artificial leg is applied, but instead of attaching it by a simple strap and leathern thigh band, it becomes requisite to create an artificial solid connection between the thigh and wooden sheath; this is done by two lateral steel uprights, furnished with a stop knee joint,* and attached to the circumference of the thigh by a semi-circular band of light metal passing at the back of the leg, about the centre of the thigh. This arrangement not only prevents the artificial leg from being withdrawn from the stump by its inherent weight, but likewise serves to impart motion to the lower leg in walking, the

* By stop is meant a check preventing the uprights from becoming more than perpendicular when the patient, in standing, places his weight in an anterior direction against the thigh band.

thigh, through the medium of the metal bars, controlling its action. Sometimes a stump, from the remains of original tenderness, &c., will be so extremely sensitive as to destroy all hope of making it a point of bearing; when this is the case (but only then as so much additional material imparts a certain amount of unnecessary clumsiness, and having to envelope the natural limb it is proportionately larger than the fellow thigh), a wooden bucket must be appended to the metal lateral uprights in lieu of the thigh band. By this means the weight of the body will be taken against the ischium as in amputation above knee. The lateral uprights should be made to slide, as it enables the patient to carefully adjust the distance between the superior edge of the lower leg sheath and the top of the bucket.

Latterly, owing to the advances made by that department of surgery called "conservative," many cases have occurred where only the anterior or tarsal portion of the foot has undergone amputation, thus leaving the os calcis or heel for the patient to rest on. This operation, although producing an extremely valuable stump for the purpose intended, becomes a matter of extreme difficulty to the "mechanician" when it has to be made the point of attachment for an artificial foot. The mechanical obstacles will be readily understood from a slight description of what has to be contrived.

In the first place, it is necessary to give the form of the anterior portion of the foot, and, having given it, to fix it in such a manner as to prevent pressure against the front of the stump when brought into action by walking. The heel being extant, it becomes evident that whatever is attached must be in contact with it, and when it is remembered that the stump presents a shape like an irregular ball, it will at once be seen that unless the artificial foot is prevented from uprising beyond a line horizontal with the ground, the resistance must necessarily fall against the front and tender end of the stump. The plan adopted by the writer in constructing an apparatus for a stump of this kind, is to sink the rounded heel into a very light and thin socket, the groundwork of which being a metal plate, the size and form of the natural sole. Rising laterally, and on both sides from this, are two light metal stems having at the ankle what is called a stop joint, the reason for which will be rendered obvious when it is stated that it prevents the sole plate from rising beyond a rectangle, and yet allows the toe part to be pointed downwards when the patient assumes a sitting position.

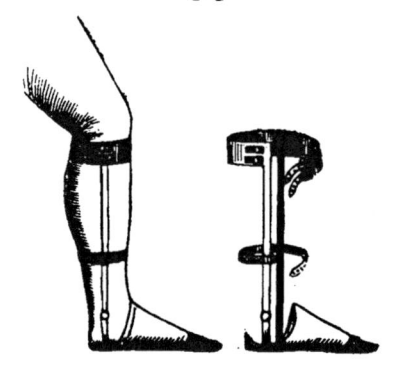

FORM OF FOOT APPARATUS. 35

Fixed to the front of the sole plate and upon its upper surface, is an artificial two-thirds foot, having a toe joint, and hollowed in that portion which rests against the anterior extremity of stump. The whole is carefully padded and fixed on to the ankle by two narrow straps. Upon the patient (wearing one of these apparati) attempting to walk, he will find the rolling action of the stump checked by the ankle band, which transferring the resistive force to the sole plate, brings the toe joint into play, and creates a natural action without the slightest pressure upon the front of the stump. If the end is at all tender, an air cushion fitted to the heel cavity may be introduced.

This is the only kind of appliance calculated

to be of much service in such cases ; but, for those patients who do not value appearance, and merely seek for such mechanical aid as will assist locomotion, a leathern hood bearing no inapt resemblance to an elephant's foot, can easily be made, and the walking rendered perfect, although rather stump-like.

SURFACE UPON WHICH THE WEIGHT OF THE BODY SHOULD BE BORNE.

As in a leg above knee one particular point is selected to sustain the weight of the patient's body, so in an artificial leg below, it becomes a matter of much importance to discover what portion of the interior of the socket is best adapted to receive the resistance of the limb. Upon carefully examining the form of the knee, it will be found that two lateral bony prominences exist just below the axis of the joint ; these are termed the condyles, and are formed by the head of the tibia, or leg bone. If these osseous tuberosities are firmly compressed, very little inconvenience is experienced by the patient upon placing his weight on such restriction ; but if the same amount of retention be directed against the anterior part of the stump, a straining uneasiness of the flesh against the end of the bone is immediately felt.

It hence becomes clearly apparent that the distribution of resistance must be over the former surface, and the conformation of the interior of the socket be made to correspond with this rule, as upon so doing, very little, if any uplifting friction can take place against the end of stump. Having determined this point, the question will undoubtedly arise as to whether a surface consisting of bone with but slight integumentary covering, can be made to sustain *for the necessary lengthened period,* pressure proceeding from a wooden ring, however accurately adjusted to it. This difficulty is, however, easily set at rest by any plan which, without interfering with the special points of bearing embraced in the shape of the sheath, shall give an artificial covering to the hard parts of the knee. This is accomplished by the insertion of a leathern cap carefully lined with a stratum of rather thick chamois skin, and placed between the knee and the inner surface of the wooden leg, which leathern cap being open at the lower end, does not in the slightest degree interfere with the freedom of the stump, but, on the contrary, rather tends, by holding the muscular covering of the leg firmly together, to encourage any movement within the socket the stump may need for its coolness and comfort.

The cap just mentioned is by no means universally adopted, but the establishment to which the writer belongs having, during a period of sixty years, employed it, and found it of extreme value, advise its being always used, the more especially as every particle of friction takes place between the cap and the wooden sheath, instead of between the latter and the stump, which circumstance would inevitably occur if it were not for the cap.

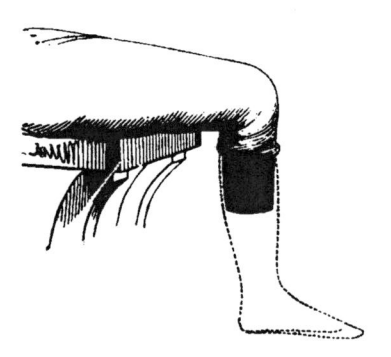

To show the extreme amount of difficulty

occasionally encountered in having to construct artificial limbs below knee, and the importance of preventing the stump from becoming angularly contracted during the time of healing, the following case is adduced.

Mr. W * * having whilst in Canada suffered from frost-bite, by which amputation of both legs became necessary, the surgeon who performed the operation very wisely determined to save, if possible, the motion of the knee joint, but in so doing left but two inches of stump on one leg and three on the other.

From the shortness of the attaching surface, and the want of mechanical skill on the part of the Canadian artisans, the laudable attempt of the surgeon to make useful joints was prevented, and a couple of artificial legs, with troughs to receive the bent knees, were constructed; the result being that although the patient was enabled to walk, yet upon sitting down, the legs thrust themselves out before him in a most inconvenient and distressing manner, and the stumps also became angularly contracted.

Upon the patient visiting London, Mr. Fergusson, of George Street, Hanover Square, sent him to the writer, considering it practicable that the stumps which had become firmly contracted at right angles, might by mechanical power be straightened, and afterwards admit of a properly constructed pair of artificial legs being applied. Mr. Fergusson kindly suggested the mechanical mode by which this might be accomplished, which consisted of two lateral bars of metal furnished with a hinged centre whose angle could be varied by the insertion of a small screw. At the inferior end of these levers a metal band corresponding to the distance existing between the under part of the knee and the end of the stump was affixed, and in front passing directly across the centre of the patella, a strong and well padded leathern band, joined one upright

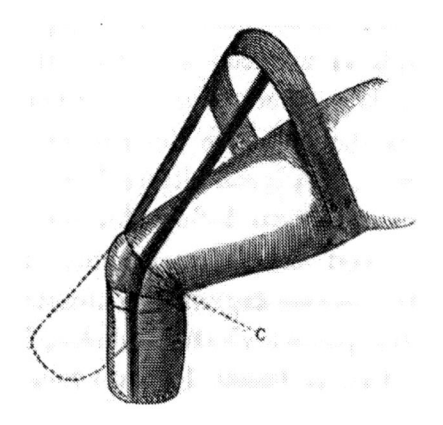

to the other. When in position the apparatus had the preceding form, which admitted of angular variation by means of the perforated disc, and screw, C.

It will at once be readily seen that upon any attempt being made to bring the lateral uprights close to the thigh in a downward direction, the force of resistance becomes transferred to the patella strap, and from thence to the metal band at the back of the stump, thus uplifting it. This mode of treatment carefully carried out by Mr. Fergusson, although occupying two or three months, answered eventually in the most perfect manner, and at this moment the patient walks well and easily, aided merely by a stick, more to prevent an accidental disturbance of his balance by slippery surface or accidental collision, than for the purpose of helping his walking. No boon could possibly be greater than enabling a patient to walk well under such circumstances as just detailed, and it serves to prove what care and ingenuity can accomplish, however difficult the conditions of the case may appear.

With this illustration of the practicability of rendering any variety of stump useful for the purpose of affixing an artificial leg, the preceding remarks are brought to a conclusion, the writer trusting he has rendered intelligible the hints intended to be conveyed to those patients who, having lost their natural limbs, desire to obtain the closest approximation in form and action when adopting artificial ones.

PART II.

ARTIFICIAL HANDS AND ARMS.

CHAPTER I.

Introductory remarks—Artificial hands and arms—Novel plan for gaining finger motion by a column of mercury—Artificial arms—Form of stump—Conical stump—Stump thickened at its end—best form of stump for mechanical attachment.

THE question is frequently asked by patients who have had the misfortune to lose either a leg or an arm, Which deprivation is the one of least importance? This point can only be decided by referring to the individual pursuits or requirements of the sufferer. So wonderfully constructed is the frame of man that he but ill spares the absence of its slightest member, all having their especial use and office ; yet there are certain positions in life where the one is more easily dispensed with than the other ; as, for instance, a carpenter, a smith, or a draughtsman, requires essentially the use of his hand, and *could* manage to carry on his usual avocations if deprived of a leg, whilst the Irish hod-carrier, a messenger or a porter, depends entirely upon the retention of his lower limbs to enable him to fulfil his customary labour. Where, however, as in the higher classes of life, it becomes requisite to conceal the loss, in addition to obtaining a certain amount of usefulness from any artificial substitute, there can be but little doubt that the absence of a hand is far preferable. The desire to hide any bodily deformity from the eyes of the world, generally imposes a difficult task upon the mechanician, who is required to combine usefulness with appearance, and thus render an artificial hand symmetrically perfect in external form, whilst capable of fulfilling certain conditions required to make it resemble in action, as well as shape, the natural limb.

The mechanical motions of a hand being much

more numerous than those required in the imitation of the lower extremities, great painstaking has to be exercised in order to render their action as nearly resembling nature as it is possible for art to do, and at the same time combine as much usefulness as inert matter has the power of fulfilling, when conformed to certain shapes resembling natural surfaces.

For this purpose various attempts have been made to impart life-like motion to the fingers of artificial hands, but without any exception such plans have invariably proved failures, and it still remains necessary in the employment of an artificial hand, for the wearer to place, by means of the natural hand, the fingers in the position they are intended to assume.

One way by which a certain amount of motion has been obtained, is that of having a minute cord passed through each finger, and terminated in one general centre a little above the wrist; this latter point being drawn upwards towards the elbow, produces a closing action in the joints, and upon the cords being relaxed; small springs placed on the upper surface of the fingers, restores them to their original position; an arrangement, however, not only subject to get continually out of order, but from the mechanical necessity of placing the cords as far away from the centre of each joint, and towards the palmar surface of the hand as possible, necessitating the joints being rendered thicker and more clumsy than is at all consonant with the usual ideas of symmetric proportion. The writer some years since devised a hand which, by a series of concealed cords and springs, possessed the power of grasping and retaining, with some slight amount of force, any light substance placed within its contact, the governing power being the fall of a small column of mercury placed in a tube within the arm part of the apparatus; the intention of which was that, upon the elbow being flexed, and the lower arm placed at an inclined plane, the gravity of the quicksilver acting upon a kind of plug to which the centre cord was attached, should at once produce a closing of the fingers, whilst the return of the mercury to the lower end of the tube, upon the arm being lowered, permitted slight springs to bring back the fingers to their original starting point. This plan, although apparently exceedingly ingenious, did not perfectly succeed, as the joints had to be made so loose that they gained lateral motion, thus conveying anything but a natural appearance to the fingers, and the liquid metal, in spite of every care taken to secure it, continually escaping, rendered useless the contrivance.

It is, therefore, only hands and arms so framed as to derive their motion from external force, that the following pages are intended to describe.

ARTIFICIAL ARMS.

In the construction of an artificial arm, the necessity for creating a surface that shall receive the weight of the body, is altogether unneeded, the object to be attained consisting more in delicacy of action and perfection of external appearance than anything assisting bodily locomotion. Although this may be considered to simplify if not entirely remove much of the mechanician's manipulative difficulties, still the skilful production of a "false arm," is a matter requiring much scientific reflection and care, both on account of the number of articular surfaces and necessity for rendering them as immediate in their action as possible.

Before entering, however, into a detailed description of the various kinds of apparati contrived for the purpose of fulfilling the office of the human arm, a few remarks upon the form and condition of the stump required for mechanical reasons, may not be unacceptable to the reader.

An arm is said to have been lost above elbow when the amputation has removed all but a certain portion of the humerus or upper arm bone. Various circumstances determine at what particular point the stump ought to terminate, although for practical use and mechanical value at least, one third of the upper arm should remain. Too great an amount of stump has been considered by many eminent surgeons to be highly objectionable on account of the tendency created by muscular traction during the healing of the cicatrix, to form a conical end, than which nothing can be more productive of difficulty to the mechanician, as from the slight integumentary covering with which the end of the bone is clothed, friction against the arm sheath is easily induced.

Likewise attended with trouble to the arm-maker is a stump thickened at its end, this being occasionally produced by the operation having taken place in the fleshy centre of an arm, particularly large and muscular.

The best shape a stump above elbow can possibly possess, is, when it *gradually* tapers from the shoulder to its end, leaving a rounded surface at its inferior extremity. An amputation above elbow may, however, take place without leaving any stump at all, this being known by its special name as " excision of the arm at the shoulder joint." The only surface of attachment in this case for an artificial appliance, is the top of the shoulder and side of the thorax or chest, which although the worst that has to be encountered in constructing artificial arms, &c., inasmuch as it is incapable of imparting motion, yet admits of being encased within such a receptacle as to defy the detection of an observer who simply employs his eyes in the investigation.

When the limb has been removed at any point of the ulna and radius, or lower arm bones, the term given is amputation below elbow. The most advantageous stump resulting from such an operation, is when two-thirds of the lower arm remain, as the leverage gained is sufficient to render useful any contrivance applied to its surface, and yet not so great as to interfere with the mechanism required to govern the action of the wrist joint. Sometimes from some particular reason, better understood by the surgeon than the mechanician, the hand is removed at the wrist joint leaving a long and difficult stump to affix any after contrivance to. A description will, however, be found given of this kind of apparatus, as well as those for every other variety in the shape and character of the stump.

CHAPTER II.

Various contrivances employed after amputation of stump above elbow—Improved shape of stump sheath—Angular motion at elbow joint—Excision of arm at shoulder joint—Arms below elbow—Form of sheath—Common arm—Short stump and apparatus—Conservative surgery—Preservation of articular surfaces—Amputation of thumb or fingers—Apparatus.

THE simplest form of apparatus for supplying the loss of an arm above elbow, is composed of a leathern sheath accurately fitted to the superior extremity of the stump. The lower end of this tubular covering is furnished with a wooden block and metal screw plate, capable of containing a fork for holding meat, a hook for carrying a weight, or a knife for cutting food. The following illustration represents its shape, with an improved appearance, the writer has for some time considered advantageous to add, as

IMPROVED SHAPE OF STUMP SHEATH.

being superior to the old fashioned form of "common arm," to explain which it is necessary to remark, that until the last few years, the line of direction between the remaining portion of the arm and its leathern covering was strictly adopted (as in the first figure), without the least disposition to follow the graceful curve inwards possessed by a natural limb. If reference be made to the drawing, it will be perceived that (in the second figure) a slight bend is imparted to the elbow which removes that stiff and uncouth appearance hitherto pertaining to a common leather arm above elbow.

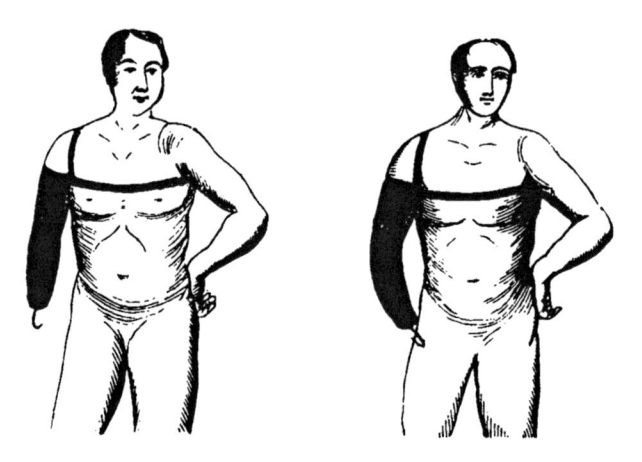

Next in progression towards the perfect representation of a natural hand and arm, is a form admitting of angular motion at the elbow communicatable at the will of the patient, and produced by a ratchet and cog-wheel concealed within its centre. The action being limited by a small spring button placed on the inner side of arm just above the elbow. (A).

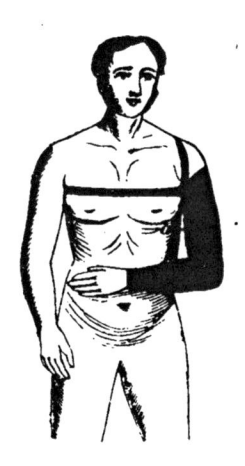

The advantage resulting from this kind of arrangement is very considerable, as it not only greatly improves the appearance of the arm, but admits of any substance like a cloak, &c., being borne upon it.

A third form is obtained by adding to the end of the leathern sheath a wooden hand, the fingers of which, although incapable of being placed in motion, still presenting an approach to natural shape, convey an infinitely better appearance than when a mere metal hook terminates the inferior extremity of the arm. It is as well to state that a hook or fork can be added to the hand part by fixing either of them in its palmar centre, which renders the apparatus highly complete, and of great value to any one not wishing to go to the expense of a more complicated piece of mechanism. One of these three descriptions of artificial arms is most generally employed after amputation of the arm above elbow, unless the limb has been removed from the shoulder joint, when a variation in form is required suitable to the particular condition offered by the entire absence of an arm stump; this apparatus consists of a soft leathern cap, or covering enveloping the whole of the top of the shoulder, and terminating at the centre of the sternum or chest bone in front, and the middle of the vertebræ or spine behind. To this cap a skilfully formed sheath is attached, possessing at its elbow-centre a ratchet joint, and at the wrist either a plate for hook, &c., or a mode of securing an artificial hand (a description of which appendage will be hereafter given), which when carefully adjusted possesses not only the action of the elbow joint but also that of the wrist in its several motions of pronation, supination, and rotation.

There is one drawback attendant upon the application of arms above elbow, regardless altogether of their form and description, to which those below are unsubject, which is the absence of the human elbow joint, as it necessitates the angle of the arm being fixed by the external action of the remaining hand, and imparts a certain amount of unavoidable stiffness. Nevertheless, independent of this disadvantage, the appearance of a well made apparatus, when fixed at a familiar angle and shaped to a natural form, presents such immense superiority over an empty sleeve that every one gladly exchanges the one for the other, and rarely returns to the appearance first following amputation.

ARMS BELOW ELBOW.

The contrivances for representing a natural hand and arm below elbow are easily enumerated and described.

56 STUMP OR COMMON ARM.

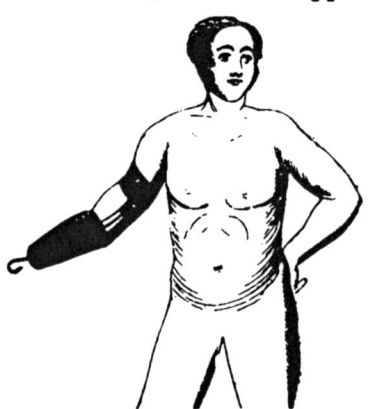

Like the different mechanical apparati recently mentioned, primary attachment to the stump is obtained by a carefully moulded leathern sheath, having its origin or surface of fixture just below the elbow. Great ingenuity is required in properly constructing this part of the apparatus, as the amount of motion naturally exercised by the elbow being but triflingly if in any degree impaired, it becomes important to offer as little impediment as possible to its action, and yet at the same time secure such protection for the extreme end of the stump as may prevent its sustaining any undue pressure or injury when the remaining part of the artificial arm is added, and brought into use. It is likewise necessary that the upper edge of the sheath should be so formed as not to interfere with the angular action of the elbow. When these considerations are attended to the patient will feel the inner part of the sheath to be in apposition with the body of the stump, whilst the end remains free and untouched, and that the movement of the elbow joint can take place without obstacle.

This elementary form constitutes, with the addition of a wooden block and screw plate, a common arm below elbow, which, when applied, is prevented from being withdrawn from the stump by a couple of lateral straps fixed to its superior edge, and terminated by a padded band placed around the upper arm.

Occasionally the stump, instead of presenting sufficient surface to ensure perfect attachment between itself and the artificial receptacle, is so short that only two inches remain for mechanical fixture. When this occurs the holding surface of the sheath is prolonged by adding two lateral metal stems jointed at the elbow, and firmly fixed to the upper arm by a well padded metal band encircling it about four inches above the axis of the joint. This arrangement transfers to the upper arm any withdrawing force applied to the stump, and consequently admits of a reasonable weight being borne by the instruments affixed to the sheath without fear of displacing its proper position.

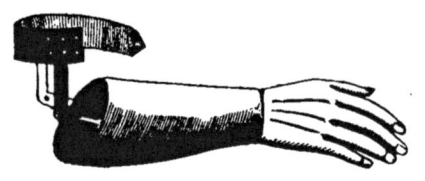

Since the introduction of "Conservative surgery" the object principally made a matter of consideration by the surgeon, being less the mechanical facilities offered by a simple stump, than the practical advantages resulting from the existence of as large a quantity of natural substance as can be obtained, after the removal of the diseased or wounded part, it follows that cases of extreme difficulty present themselves to the eye of the mechanician. In all, or with few exceptions, nothing can be urged in opposition to the immense advantage attained by the existence of a large amount of muscular motion, often accompanied by the saving of articular surfaces, still, although the boon be present, it is a matter of considerable trouble to render it scientifically useful; thus, in cases where but a thumb and small portion of the meta carpal bones remain, the impression invariably exists that action of the wrist joint may be preserved in any mechanical adaptation. Such a desideratum *can* be carried out, but it demands great skill and ingenuity to effect it, as may be judged by a description of the apparatus. A leathern covering is first conformed to the stump with an aperture to allow of the thumb passing through, and an open space along its entire length in order to admit the thickened end of stump past the wrist, which it would not otherwise do from the diameter of the hand being greater than the wrist. At the inferior extremity artificial fingers jointed to represent the other hand are affixed, and at the wrist a small metallic joint, curved in a particular manner, enables the action of the wrist to be maintained thus :—

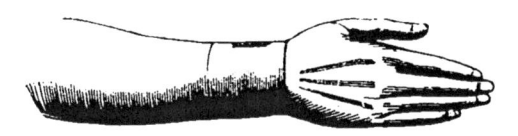

This contrivance both retains the action of the wrist, and enables the patient to present a tolerably well-formed hand.

The preservation of the thumb in such cases as these, proves of the highest value, and too much praise cannot be given to the eminent surgeons who first introduced, and now practise, this particular mode of operation.

There are many other forms of stump besides these; but the mechanical apparati being merely modifications of what have already been described, need no particular statement of their shape and form.

CHAPTER III.

Artificial fingers and hand—Mechanical motion—Form of hand—Softening of surface—Form of joint—Ginglymoid joint described—Position of mechanical axis in fingers and thumb—Form of wrist—Spring in thumb joint.

IN the contrivances hitherto described for supplying the deficiency produced by the loss of an arm, but little has been said of the mechanism employed to give form and motion to the hand and fingers. Where, however, external similitude is as much valued as practical utility, the existence of a perfectly symmetric artificial hand becomes highly desirable, and an invariable amount of regret is created by a knowledge of the impossibility of simulating, with anything approaching to exactitude, the delicate warmth and softness bestowed by nature. With this exception, nothing can be more entitled to praise as a piece of imitative art, than a well-constructed mechanical hand.

What, however, it lacks in delicacy of touch it gains in artistic proportion ; as it by no means unfrequently happens that the wearer becomes so delighted with the regular outline of the artificial hand as to prefer its gloved surface being seen in lieu of the remaining natural member. Yet it must not be supposed that want of similarity exists between the two hands more than sufficient to prevent any trifling irregularity in the profile of the natural fingers being obtrusively followed in the artificial resemblance.

Attempts have been made to soften the surface by placing a covering of gutta percha and india rubber over the material composing it; but in spite of such precaution touch instantly decides between the real hand and its counterfeit.

There are, however, means by which the extreme hardness of the substance employed in its construction may be much diminished, and as it requires but a very slight amount of tact on the part of the patient to present the natural hand, whenever it is likely to be touched, this condition fulfils all that is needed, and enables the wearer to defy detection.

In order to comprehend the principles upon which an artificial hand is constructed, it is requisite for the reader to carefully consider the motion of a hand when the fingers are being closed by muscular effort; and he will at once perceive that the mechanical form of the joints is that termed ginglymoid, or hinged. But if the same hand, whilst so closing, be placed upon or made to grasp a globular surface, rather larger than its own concavity, the fingers will be seen to expand laterally, and conform themselves to the increased space. It will thus appear that what the mechanician has to accomplish in making an artificial hand, is to obtain these two movements, viz. angular motion in the same plane, as the fingers move downwards, and lateral motion rectangular to such plane.

But upon attempting to carry these apparently simple conditions into effect, it will at once be found that only one of the two motions admit of perfect accomplishment; no joint but a ball and socket being capable of moving in more than one plane at the same moment, and the ball and socket, on account of the impossibility of maintaining the requisite amount of control over its movement, is rendered thoroughly inadmissible.

The form of finger joint thus necessarily becomes the hinged or ginglymoid, the axes of which must correspond to those previously existing in the natural hand, and, therefore in the case of the thumb, placed at right angles to the others, its office being to close itself against the fingers, which it could not effect unless the mechanical action took its proximate rise in a lateral direction. To the natural thumb a third action pertains, viz., an uplifting of itself against the inner side of the fingers ; this, in the substitute, is mechanically accomplished by a small hinged spring placed between the base of the thumb and fingers, thus giving it two distinct planes of motion, which, in placing a glove upon the artificial hand, is found highly advantageous admitting, as it does, of a lessening in the size of that portion which represents the thickest part.

In using the natural hand in the manner previously stated (grasping a ball), an important part of its action will be found dependent upon the motion of the wrist, which thus directs the employment of similar mechanism in the construction of the substitute. The wrist possesses three distinct actions, one corresponding to the plane of the fingers, and enabling the hand to be extended laterally, a second producing rotation, and a third admitting of a hinge-like motion; the two latter being by far the most important are especially simulated in an artificial wrist joint, the mechanical method of accomplishment being by furnishing the posterior extremity of the hand with a metal plate in the centre of which a "key-hole plug" is affixed. Corresponding to this, but on a plate fixed to the end of the arm sheath, is an aperture of similar shape, the two fitting each other most accurately and the plug being so constructed as to have a trifling prominence at its end, which, upon slightly turning after the two are placed together, prevents separation during rotation. The only time the two surfaces can part is when the projection on the plug A. and the key-hole slit of the aperture B. become coincident; this occurring but once during an entire revolution of the wrist plate secures perfect axial rotation.

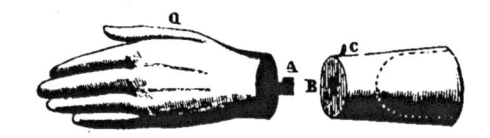

A small spring acting against a certain number of holes or depressions in the wrist plate, limits the amount of circular motion, and permits the hand to be placed in any natural position. The other action of the wrist is obtained by a joint composed of a shallow cup (or glenoid cavity) and semi-spherical tenon, the centre of which is secured by a pin passing from the wrist plate. When these several pieces of mechanism are combined a most perfect representation of the action of the human wrist results.

The most modern improvement applied to the hand is an attachment of a spring within the centre of the thumb, D, the office of which is to secure a certain amount of resistive force between itself and the fore-finger, thus enabling any reasonable weight to be held between them, and affording the patient the power of tying his neckerchief, holding a pen, or paper, &c.

An artificial hand, however, would be but a matter of ornament were it not that means exist for the attachment of such apparati as serve by their action to imitate the uses to which a natural hand is ordinarily applied; but as these instruments are very various, they will be found detailed according to their several degrees of importance, it only being requisite to state that a small steel socket or receptacle exists in the palm of every well made artificial hand for the fixture of such appliances.

CHAPTER IV.

Instruments for artificial hand—Hook—Driving hook—Holding gun—Lifting weights—Fork for holding food—Pen holder—Nail brush—Penknife—Ring for spade or agricultural implements—Dagger or weapon for defence—Instructions for taking measure of leg or arm—Conclusion.

As in the construction of false fingers it is requisite to allow them to retain enough freedom in their action to admit of being placed in position by the pressure of the remaining hand, it follows that they are necessarily incapable of sustaining in their grasp any substance possessing weight, it is therefore needful to employ some contrivance by which the usual office of the hand can be fulfilled, such as lifting a chair, holding a pencil, pen, or pack of cards, carving a joint, driving, &c., for which purposes various apparati are made.

The following is a slight description of the most useful.

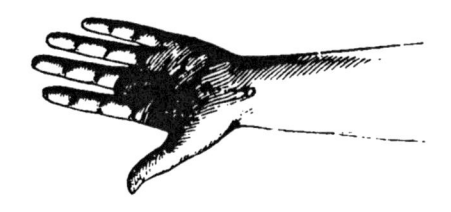

Fig. A. represents a simple hook with spring fastening, by which it can be secured to the palm of the hand, and removed from it at pleasure.

The office of the hook is important when applied to an artificial hand, in enabling it to fulfil any act of ordinary lifting, &c. It has various modifications, such as the driving hook, which, composed of a double tenaculum, admits of the reins being separated, and thus held in the same position as they would be by the natural fingers.

Loss of the hand by gun explosion is not only of exceedingly frequent occurrence, but it also often happens that the remembrance of the accident is insufficient to quench the desire of the sportsman for a renewal of his amusement. This when the right hand still remains is easily accomplished by affixing to his artificial hand a hook so shaped as to hold the barrel of the gun.

Another kind of hook is one capable of being fastened to the arm-plate, and intended for lifting heavy weights, as being used when the artificial hand is removed, it allows the whole stress to be borne by the muscles of the arm.

Amongst the most important instruments for enabling an artificial hand to simulate the power possessed by its natural prototype, a fork for holding meat must not be overlooked, as however gladly a patient repudiates the necessity for lifting weights, &c., few feel inclined to admit that a fork to retain the food whilst divided by a knife in the opposite hand is at all unneeded. When the stump is short, a certain amount of difficulty occurs to the patient in getting the fork to the mouth, but if a particular set or shape be given to its stem, this can at once be easily overcome.

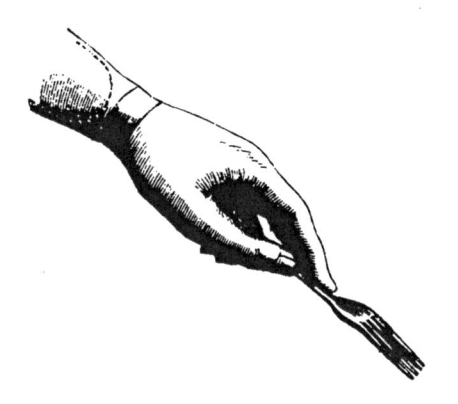

If the right hand be lost, it becomes necessary to furnish some mechanical means for enabling the wearer of an artificial arm, to employ his pen, for which purpose, a metal holder inserted into the palm of the hand, has been devised, and by its aid the patient can grasp a pen with sufficient power to write tolerably well.

If, however, the hand has a spring thumb, the pen holder is not so much required, as the first and second fingers retain a pen pressed against them by the thumb sufficiently well to impress its marks upon paper, and consequently write with a tolerable amount of firmness.

A brush for cleansing the nails can also be attached to the palm of the hand, as likewise a file with penknife at its extremity, the blade of which standing rectangularly to the surface of the file, enables the nails of the natural fingers to be easily pared.

For horticultural purposes, a pruning knife is occasionally appended as also a ring for holding the handle of a hoe or rake, this latter apparatus

WEAPON FOR DEFENCE. 73

being made with three joints, permits of the rake handle being moved in any direction.

A few years since, the writer was applied to by a patient who requested to be furnished with a dagger blade attached to his stump sheath. Though rather a remarkable desire it ultimately proved of great value, by enabling the gentleman to defend himself against the attack of any wild animal he might in his travels encounter ; and as his pursuit was that of collecting furs for the Hudson Bay Company, such precaution was highly necessary. The following is a drawing of the weapon and its mode of attachment.

The number and variety of instruments capable of being applied to an artificial hand admits of scarcely any limit, as whatever the human limb is capable of performing can be readily accomplished by skilfully-contrived mechanical aid. Sufficient general idea has, however, been given by the preceding wood-cuts to enable any one requiring such appliances to fully understand their form and method of application.

METHOD BY WHICH THE DIMENSIONS OF A STUMP EITHER FOR ARTIFICIAL LEG OR ARM CAN BE ACCURATELY TAKEN.

The object the writer has had in view during the foregoing pages being to bring within the comprehension of his readers a knowledge of the various forms of artificial limbs and their adaptation to the human body, he is especially desirous of furnishing such patients who either by residing a long distance from London or possessing infirm health are denied the power of practically investigating the advantages belonging to scientifically constructed apparati with a means of testing the accuracy of the rules laid down for their guidance. For this purpose he appends directions by following which an exact description of the stump and shape of remaining leg can be easily conveyed.

In making a leg, the dimensions *positively* requisite are the circumference of the stump close up to the fork or perinæum and the distance from the perinæum to the ground, accompanied as a kind of check by the length from the centre of knee-joint (or inner condyle) to the ground where the heel rests. Whilst, however, these measurements are being obtained it is very little additional trouble for the patient to take, or have taken, a few other dimensions indicative of the muscular thickness possessed by the calf or delicate thinness belonging to the ankle. It is, therefore, advisable to proceed in the following manner.

FOR A LEG OF ANY ARTIFICIAL FORM.

Let the patient be placed in a sitting posture upon the ground, having under him two large sheets of brown paper, pinned together at their edges to make up the required length.

Upon these the profile of the remaining leg and stump can be marked.

76 INSTRUCTION FOR TAKING MEASUREMENT.

Pass a tape measure round the top of thigh, A., centre of thigh, B., centre of knee, C., centre of calf, D, centre of ankle, E, placing the number of inches upon the paper opposite each of these spots of circumference. Take also the size of the stump at its upper part, G, around

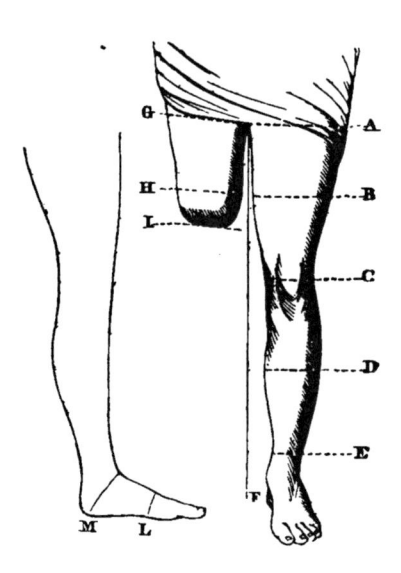

its centre, H, at its extreme end, I. Likewise the perpendicular length from perinæum to ground, F, and perinæum to end of stump.

Having carefully done this, turn the paper over to its opposite side and place the remain-

INSTRUCTION FOR TAKING MEASUREMENT. 77

ing leg in a bent position sidelong upon it, Fig. 2, marking the profile as before, but taking only the circumference of the heel and instep, M, and the toes, L.

This process enables the axis of each joint to be exactly ascertained.

If the leg has been lost below knee, place the patient likewise in a SITTING position upon the floor, with the paper and mark the profile of both leg and stump, commencing the circumferential measurement just below the patella or knee-cap, A, take size of calf, B, ankle, C, and two circumferences of the stump, D and E, also the perpendicular distances, F F, and G G.

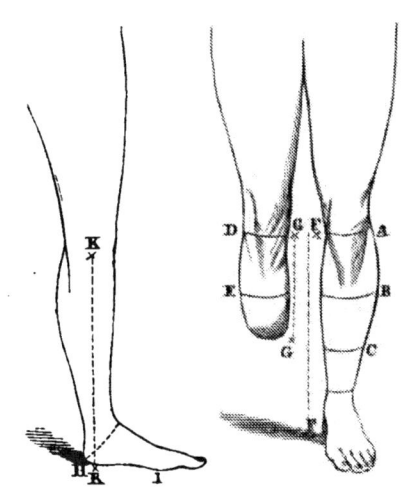

Reverse the surface of paper and take the leg in a bent position, making the heel and instep, H, and perpendicular distance from inner condyle or knee bone to bottom of calcis or heel K. It is also better in addition to place the sole of the foot on paper whilst the patient is standing, and mark its form.

FOR AN ARTIFICIAL HAND AND ARM.

In taking the shape of an arm, &c., the hand must be placed upon paper with its fingers extended, and the profile taken by a thin pencil which in order to avoid enlarging the size of fingers should be held perfectly upright. Against each finger joint a small mark must be made indicating its centre of movement, C, D, E, F, G.

The stump must be carefully drawn with its circumference placed in inches upon the paper, as at B, A. It is also requisite to have furnished, a correct measure of the arm requiring an artificial hand, taken just above the elbow, as this gives the size of the strap required to support the arm sheath on the stump.

With these instructions the patient can be

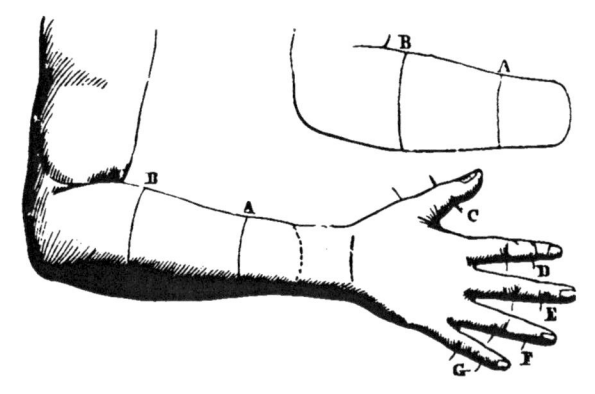

readily furnished with the required contrivances and receive every advantage possible to attain from the employment of artificial aid, at the same time avoiding the expense of a visit to London.

The writer in bringing to a conclusion his remarks upon the advantageous utility of artificial limbs, fully trusts that his endeavours will find appreciation at the hands of those who require adventitious aid, and ventures to indulge a hope that he has not overrated the amount of ingenuity and intelligence required to enable such apparati to prove alike meritorious to himself and beneficial to the patients adopting his suggestions.

FINIS.

Anatomical, Surgical, and Orthopædic Appliances,

CONTRIVED, MANUFACTURED, AND SUPPLIED BY

HENRY HEATHER BIGG,

29, LEICESTER SQUARE, LONDON.

Owing to the advances made in the treatment of deformity, by the introduction of tenotomy (or surgical division of the tendons), and the consequent attention bestowed by the Medical Profession upon the subject, the construction of mechanical apparati has been rendered a business of great scientific merit requiring not only a knowledge of the anatomical changes that occur in the production of malformity, but also a comprehensive understanding of the mechanical forces to be employed in overcoming such disturbance.

The Scarpa shoe (abounding as it does with erroneous mechanism), and tin splint, no longer constitute the only kind of apparatus for the cure of club foot, nor the backboard and collar remain the best means for treating spinal curvature.

Experience and an acquaintance with modern science have succeeded in proving that in order to obtain with certainty the removal of deformity, such anatomical instruments as may be necessary to employ, must be proximately conformed to the individual peculiarities of each case.

It is with this view that the following appliances are offered to the attention of the Medical Profession, as serving to illustrate the different forms of apparati contrived to enable them to treat with success any case that may arise in ordinary practice, not one instrument is mentioned which has not received the approval of the most eminent surgeons, and almost all owe perfection to their valuable suggestions.

ORTHOPŒDIC INSTRUMENTS FOR TALIPES, OR CLUB FOOT.

VARUS.

1. An improved "Scarpa shoe," with compound rack and pinion movement, corresponding in motion to the inversion of the toes, contraction of the heel, and *rotation of anterior part of the foot.*

2. A padded tin splint, generally used for infantile

cases, after the division of the tibial tendons, and before operating on the tendo achilles, when a modification of the "improved Scarpa shoe," is needed.

3. An apparatus governed by vulcanized elastic cords (so placed as to antagonize the contracted tendons), and possessing the advantage of permitting muscular motion, whilst the treatment is proceeding, the centres of action also corresponding perfectly with those of the limb.

4. A retentive apparatus with double stop joint to be worn after the foot is reduced to its natural position, or at night.

VALGUS.

An apparatus strictly resembling in outward form an ordinary boot, but capable, by means of an india-rubber pad, of uplifting the arch of the foot, and producing lateral support against the tarsus.

EQUINUS.

1. An instrument consisting of a metal shoe, with single rack and pinion joint, corresponding to the axis of the malleoli or ankle joint.

2. A metal shoe, and two lateral curved levers with a connecting strap to press upon the instep—this apparatus is called "Liston's shoe."

3. Stromeyer's foot board and pulleys.

DEFORMITY OF THE LEGS.

CURVED TIBIA, OR BOWED-LEGS.

1. A padded wooden splint, with straps and buckles to fix it against the inside of the leg, and a metal socket to secure it to the boot.

2. An instrument attached to a common boot, and consisting of a metal stem on the inside of the leg from the knee downwards—a thin metal trough at the back of the calf and ankle—a padded strap to depress the anterior curve, and a broad lacing band to overcome the lateral deviation.

GENU VALGUM, OR KNOCKED-KNEES.

1. A padded splint with hip and ankle joints, extending from the pelvis downwards and attached to the legs by padded webbing bands, also fixing in the boot by means of a metal socket.

2. Light metal stems, furnished with ankle, knee- and hip joints, the abduction of the knee being overcome by padded straps.

3. A padded splint without joints to be worn at night.

CURVED FEMUR.

A stem from hip to heel outside of the leg, with a metal band pressing upon the front of the thigh.

KNOCK KNEES AND BOWED LEGS.

An instrument descending from the hip to the centre of the knee on the outside of leg, and from knee to heel on the inside of the leg, with straps and lacing bandage to overcome tibial curvature, and inward deflection of the knee.

CONTRACTED AND DISEASED HIP.

1. An apparatus with rack and pinion joints, capable of producing the motions of extension, abduction, and rotation.

2. An instrument governed by vulcanized elastic cords, the advantage being that the patient cannot easily break the apparatus by accidentally stumbling, as sometimes happens when the joints are fixed on the rack and pinion principle.

3. A leathern splint enveloping pelvis and thigh, generally worn during the progress of disease, and being constructed with aperture for dressing the abscess, if present.

CURVATURES OF THE SPINE.

LATERAL.

So numerous are the varieties of lateral curvature that each case demands an especial modification in the construction of the apparatus. The proximate principles upon which they all are based may be classed under the following headings:—

1. Extension of the spinal column by lateral supports, passing from the pelvis to the axillæ, and upholding the body by either webbing bands or padded plates.

2. Depression of the arc of each curve by metal plates resting on the convexity and governed in their action and adjustment by rack and pinion screw centres.

3. Expansion of the extremities of each curve by uplifting the depressed side of the thorax, and supporting by padded plates the arc of the curve.

4. Torsional rotation of the ribs and vertebræ from behind forwards.

A new principle has lately been applied, by Mr. H. H. Bigg, to the construction of spinal apparati in the employment of vulcanized elastic bands (fixed to a proper spinal apparatus), which, by their peculiar action, keep up a continuous but elastic pressure against the convexities, thus preventing the patient from slipping the body away from the mechanical surface, as frequently happens with the more powerful kinds of spinal instruments, rendering the latter not only excessively weighty and clumsy, but inoperative. Another great advantage is that respiration is not in the least degree interfered with, thus no mischievous depression of the ribs upon themselves can occur, or any other injurious effect, the supports are likewise exceedingly light.

POSTERIOR.

An instrument composed of two lateral uprights affixed to a pelvic band and uplifting the whole of the superincumbent weight of the head and shoulders by taking a bearing under the arms and against the sides of the chest or thorax.

ANTERIOR.

A support having, in addition to two lateral uprights, a broad webbing band passing over the chest just below the sternum, and producing a lessening of the prominence formed by anterior lumbar curvature.

CERVICAL.

1. An apparatus with rack and pinion movement, controlling the action of the head and possessing the power of elongation, lateral deflection, and rotation.
2. An apparatus with india-rubber cords serving the same purpose.

SURGICAL AND ANATOMICAL INSTRUMENTS.

HERNIA OR RUPTURE, WITH A DESCRIPTION OF THE VARIOUS PLANS EMPLOYED FOR THE SUPPORT OF INGUINAL, SCROTAL, FEMORAL, UMBILICAL, AND VENTRAL RUPTURES.

There is no mechanical instrument contrived for the human body possessing more numerous forms than that of a bandage for rupture, ordinarily known by the name of a truss. All possess some slight amount of merit, and none are so perfect as to answer infallibly in every case. Trusses may be grouped into three classes, viz., 1st, those which support the rupture by aid of a metallic spring encircling the body. 2nd, those which employ a metallic spring in the pad; and 3rd, those that have no springs. The first is the form generally employed, and if carefully adjusted to the anatomical form of the body answers as well as any; no mistake being greater than the supposition that because a metal band passes round the hips it must necessarily imply the existence of great circumferential pressure, as, if rightly made, the only point where resistance should be actively felt is the pad which gains a steadiness and support from the metal band that nothing else ever gives to it.

The second is generally composed of a webbing band, encircling the hips, and a pad with perpendicular lever spring, the strength and action of which, when placed against the hernia, depends entirely upon the *tightness* of an understrap, at all times a great nuisance, and easily dispensed with in the ordinary truss. The third kind is an elastic belt and inflated pad, the mechanical tendency of which is based upon the supposition that if the abdominal parietes are supported, much less remains for the pad to do; this, however, is open to doubt, as it appears reasonable to infer that the additional pressure made upon the contents of the abdomen by enveloping its surface in a strong compressive (although elastic) belt tends rather to drive the intestine outwards through the inguinal ring, than aid the support given by the pad.

The best form of truss undoubtedly is a well-adjusted band around the pelvis, with a pad filled neither with air or water, but another *element*, viz., earth or sand.

This idea was first suggested by Mr. Aston Key, and has been applied in thousands of cases with excellent success—the principle appearing to depend upon the power possessed by the molecules of sand to adjust their surface accurately to that of the abdominal parietes, thus securing the desideratum of *every kind of pad*, viz., a close approximation between the surface of support and the inguinal canal. Trusses so constructed can be had for inguinal, scrotal, femoral, umbilical, ventral, or any other kind of hernia.

VARICOSE VEINS, ANASARCHOUS SWELLINGS, WEAKNESS OF THE ARTICULAR LIGAMENTS, &c.

VARICOSE VEINS—DESCRIPTION OF STOCKING, &C.

The object of every kind of bandage for varicose veins, is to supply a contractile surface of such a nature as to diminish the contents of the enlarged veins without producing painful constriction of the limb, this being accomplished by a fabric composed of india-rubber fibres interwoven with silk or cotton.

FALLACY OF THE "SPIRAL" PRINCIPLE.

Latterly an idea has existed that the stocking, &c., should be composed of a long strip of elastic material, joined together at its edges, and conformed to the shape of the limb, the *supposed* advantage being that, whilst free from seam, the contraction of the material acting on a helical principle, would cause a gradual support to diffuse itself over the entire surface; this appears reasonable enough, but unfortunately is unsustained by experience, as, instead of one slight joining (for it does not deserve the name of seam) at the back of the leg, as in an ordinary elastic stocking, every "spiral" becomes a prolonged seam acting transversely to the direction of the vein, and undoubtedly not in the slightest degree imitating the *even* surface of support afforded by the *natural integuments*, which, if the "spiral principle" were right, would most decidedly have been created in a conjoined strip, instead, as we know it to be, a general surface.

NEW PLAN OF SUPPORTING THE VEINS.

A new and valuable plan has for some little time been introduced, which consists of the employment of a small silken pad running the length of the enlarged veins, the inequality of which within the stocking produces the greatest amount of support upon the weakest surface, and consequently admits of the *enlarged veins* being made the principal point of compression.

WEAKNESS OF THE KNEE OR ANKLE JOINTS.

For anasarchous swellings, weakness of the knee or ankle joints, &c., various contrivances are applied, some consisting of an entirely elastic fabric, and others of a lacing bandage, formed of strong jean and india-rubber, as in cases requiring great support a surface almost inelastic has been found most beneficial.

PROLAPSUS UTERI, PENDULOUS ABDOMEN, WEAKNESS OF THE ABDOMINAL PARIETES, &c.

The form of apparatus usually employed for the

support of prolapsus uteri is an elastic surface corresponding to the shape of the abdomen, with an eliptical pad producing external pressure against the perinæum, thus superseding the application of pessaries.

Another plan (adopted several years) has for its object the support of the uterus, by pressure against the lower part of the abdomen, or what is termed the hypogastric region. There are several means of accomplishing this, the least serviceable being an air pad inserted beneath the lower edge of the belt, and insufflated after the bandage is applied, the objection to which is, that the pad in its expansion is much more likely to uplift the elastic belt than produce pressure of any considerable amount against the abdomen. The best way of securing such an end is by first fitting a light but strong elastic belt to the abdomen, and then increasing the pressure on the hypogastric region by fastening a laced elastic band, so made as merely to embrace the lower part of the abdomen, yet being part of the belt. This form of bandage, from its peculiar mechanical action, has obtained the name of "an abdominal uplifter."

PENDULOUS ABDOMEN.

The object necessary to carry out is that of securing an amount of support for the abdomen, by which its pendulosity shall be overcome, this being accomplished by an elastic belt, fastening with buckles at the back, and having a strong webbing strap running the entire length of its lower edge.

WEAKNESS OF THE ABDOMINAL PARIETES.

In cases where the muscles of the abdomen are relaxed or separated above or below the umbilicus (as occasionally happens), the kind of apparatus consists of an elastic belt furnished with two perpendicular pads which, upon being applied, press the surface of the abdomen towards its mesial or central line, thus bringing together the relaxed parietes.

In all contrivances intended for the support of the abdomen, elasticity combined with supporting power is the desideratum, and unless the fabric of which the belt is composed fulfils both these conditions, it is impossible the apparatus should answer its end. Of course the strength varies in proportion to the amount of support needed, as if simply intended to be applied during the time a patient is *enceinte*, the material may be lighter and much more elastic than if required for dropsy, ovarian tumour, ventral hernia, &c.

PROLAPSUS ANI.

There are several kinds of bandage for the support of prolapsus ani, the simplest being a padded belt around the pelvis, a padded perinæal strap with oval pad carried from the back part of the pelvic belt, and fastened in front, the end being bifurcated, or divided in two, for the purpose of gaining an even support from the front of the belt. A second form of bandage is a band round the pelvis containing a small strip of metal, from the centre of which a spring is affixed, which terminates at its lower extremity in an ivory pad, the object of which is to produce uplifting pressure against the anus. A third and still better plan consists in the substitution of an oval annulus or ring for the ivory pad, the inner edges of which hold a stratum of india-rubber. When this is applied the ring becomes an artificial sphincter ani, and the india-rubber septum prevents the intestine passing between its centre. It is likewise free from the objection constantly urged against an ivory pad, viz., that its hard and conical surface is continually dilating the weakened sphincter, thus increasing the malady whilst seeking to overcome its results.

The worst cases of prolapsus ani have been successfully treated by this *ring apparatus*, which is further mechanically improved by the insertion of a small screw motion at its upper edge, as the support can then be augmented or decreased at pleasure.

HYDROCELE, VARICOCELE, &c.

The form of suspender best suited for these cases is a silk net bag with a thin strip of elastic round each thigh, and another ascending from its upper edge, and fastened to any part of the patient's dress.

The advantage consists in there being no waist-band to encumber the wearer's body, and also that, as the whole bandage is elastic, it yields freely to every position the patient can assume. It likewise produces a certain amount of pressure upon the surface it is applied to, and in cases of hydrocele, &c., induces absorption of the fluid contents.

IRRETENTION.

In the distressing maladies resulting from debility of so important an organ as the bladder, mechanical means are required to lessen, as much as possible, any annoyance the patient may be subjected to by a continual escape of fluid. The apparatus consists of an india-rubber receptacle, furnished with a valve to prevent regurgitation, and a tap for the withdrawal of the fluid when needed. There are several forms given to the apparatus, as some are required to be worn at night, others merely during the day, &c. They are so contrived as to be perfectly concealed by the ordinary dress, and fit the body with the utmost exactitude.

MISCELLANEOUS CONTRIVANCES.

For contraction of the fingers or toes.—The kind of instrument employed for the fingers is a metal plate taking its bearing against the back of the hand, to which is affixed a lever the precise length of the finger contracted, and having rack and pinion motion corresponding to the axes of the joints; these, upon being straightened, produce a similar change in the surface to which they are applied, and gradually overcome the malformity. For the toes a different kind of instrument is needed, viz., a metal shoe with a lateral stem secured by buckle and strap to the leg, from the edge of the sole plate a small curved bar passes over the contracted toe, the direction of which can be changed by means of a rack and pinion joint which, when brought into play, uplifts the toe and removes the contraction.

If the case is a mild one, then a metal plate affixed to the sole of the foot, and furnished with slits for the passage of ribbon loops over the contracted toes, will generally be found to answer. Sometimes the toes, without any positive contraction, have the habit of uplifting themselves against the upper part of the boot, producing not only tenderness in the ball of the foot, but an extremely ugly appearance. This can be easily corrected by the insertion of a semi-lunar pad of india-rubber just beneath the metatarso-phalangeal articulations, which has the effect of immediately straightening the toes, and allowing the patient to walk with ease.

Bunion of the great toes.—Almost all are familiar with the disagreeable enlargement occasionally observed as affecting the joint of the great toe, and which is undoubtedly attributable in a large number of instances to the habit of wearing an unmechanically constructed boot. The name familiarly given is "a bunion," and it owes its increase to the lateral separation of the metatarso-phalangeal articulation of the great toe. The apparatus, by which this can be greatly diminished, and often entirely overcome, consists of a slight spring jointed at the toe (so that it may not interfere with the natural action), at the place where the joint occurs, an eliptical opening is formed in the instrument and that portion of the spring which is anterior to this point, curves outwards in a lateral direction. When secured to the toe, the reactive force of the spring carries the great toe outwards until it assumes its natural position and gently depresses the enlarged joint, by approximating the external articular surfaces. This little instrument is generally worn only during night-time, although it can be so constructed as to admit of being placed within an ordinary boot.

EXCISION OF THE ELBOW OR KNEE.

When the bones comprising the elbow joint, have been removed, the arm would be rendered useless were it not that an apparatus can be supplied to sustain it in position. This consists of two lateral stems curved to the angle of the arm, and attached by a band to the wrist and another to the upper arm. When the limb is in an instrument of this kind, the fingers can grasp and become of use to their owner;

in consequence of an amount of power being given to the muscles of the arm by the distension of the divided osseous surfaces. If the knee joint has been removed, then a broad thigh plate and two lateral stems fixed to the sole of the boot is the best form of instrument, as it takes the weight of the body from the knee joint and transfers it to the apparatus.

DISUNITED FEMUR, TIBIA, HUMERUS, &C.

For the thigh, a support precisely similar to that used in cases of excised knee is the best, care being taken to make the thigh band so deep as to embrace a large surface of the leg and thus keep the disunited femur from anterior displacement. For the leg, an apparatus having two lateral stems and a broad metal band taking its bearing against the condyles is the kind employed. For the arm, a thick leathern sheath firmly placed around the point of disunition, and acting as a kind of splint to keep the ends of the bones in apposition, is generally made use of.

FRACTURE OF THE PATELLA.

The object to be obtained by the employment of mechanical power, is that of keeping the edges of the fractured bone in continual contact, until either cartilaginous or osseous union has resulted. The instrument for accomplishing this is composed of two metal stems with a stop-joint in their centre, the advantage being that the knee can only flex to a very small angle, which not only prevents any separation of the fracture, but aids the pressure established by two padded straps passing anteriorly above and below the seat of injury, the whole apparatus is attached to the knee by a padded band around the thigh and another at the calf. A second form of appliance is one having a metal spring at the back of the knee and terminated by two semi lunar pads encircling the patella and keeping the fracture in a state of contact.

Splints for fractures, and bandages for dislocation are so numerous in their form and character that it is impossible to explain them as fully as they require to be done in the small space devoted to the description of miscellaneous instruments.

LUMBAR DEBILITY, OR WEAKENED LOINS.

The apparatus is of American invention, and consists of a slight spring passing around the shoulders and another over the hips, the two being joined together by a thin perpendicular metallic strip. When applied, the body becomes uplifted without in the least degree controlling its natural action.

EYE DOUCHE FOR WEAKNESS OF VISION, &C.

The effect of a continuous stream of water being allowed to play against the closed eyelids, is attended with such beneficial results to those patients who either by reading, have strained their eyesight or constitutionally suffer from irritable and weak eyes, that an apparatus has been especially contrived for such a purpose. It consists of a metallic basin, containing a measured quantity of water, and a metal syringe fixed in its centre, the valves of which are so arranged as to secure a stream without cessation, with the same degree of force and temperature, until all the fluid in the basin is exhausted.

CRUTCHES AND ARM SLINGS.

The form of a crutch more or less depends upon the circumstances under which it may be needed. Thus, if the patient is a lady who has lost her leg, or sustained any extensive injury to her limbs rendering her entirely dependent upon the stability of the support, and yet desiring the possession of as much lightness and elasticity as is consonant with its purpose, the best crutch she could have, would be one formed of a *single shaft* with an elliptical opening in its centre to admit the hand—at its head, or that part where the arm rests, should be a tubular spring, contained within a metal sheath forming part of the shaft, the advantage of which is that upon the weight of the body being placed on the crutch, it yields in a perpendicular direction, and prevents any jar against the arm-pit. In addition to this (*and which is the most recent improvement*) the head should be composed of a cushion filled with water, as it accommodates itself better than any other kind of padding to the form of the arm, and always retains its softness. Supposing the crutch to be required for a gentleman, then instead of one shaft the upper half should be double, and possess two tubular springs, having also the water cushion.

A crutch so constructed is double the strength of one made for a lady. If a crutch is required merely for a very short period, then the springs and water cushions can be dispensed with. There are also crutches made with only a straight stick and padded head. A webbing sling is occasionally attached to a crutch for the purpose of supporting the weight of the leg. For an arm sling the best form is a leathern trough containing the arm and hand, with the power of extending or contracting its length; it should be attached to the body by a silken strap, over the neck; a simpler shape is sometimes used, viz., a leathern rest just long enough to receive the middle of the arm, and a webbing strap and buckle to fix it to the patient.

⁎ The prices of the various apparati mentioned in the preceding list of contrivances, are governed entirely by the amount of mechanical labour required

for their construction, all, however, being sufficiently reasonable as to admit of purchase at a moderate cost. They can be obtained from

Mr. H. H. BIGG.

29, Leicester Square, London.